TRUCKS

OF EVERY SORT

TRUCKS
OF EVERY SORT

BY KEN ROBBINS

CROWN PUBLISHERS, INC.   NEW YORK

The text of this book is set in 12 point Bookman Light.
The illustrations are black-and-white photographs.

Library of Congress Cataloging in Publication Data
Robbins, Ken.
   Trucks of every sort.
   Summary: Text and photos describe a variety of trucks and
explain their functions.   Includes a moving van, dump truck,
ice-cream truck, and fire truck.
   1.Trucks—Juvenile literature. [1.Trucks] I.Title.
TL230.R6   1981   629.2'24   81-9791
ISBN 0-517-54164-5   AACR2

FOR MARIA

Contents

Introduction

Standing at an intersection near my home one day, I decided to count the different kinds of trucks that went by. In less than an hour I saw trucks carrying bulldozers, ice cream, shoe polish, potato chips, gasoline, garbage, rocks, sand, water, milk, bread, television sets, clothes, furniture, ribbon, horses, scissors, concrete, watches, houses, fence posts, salami, and newspapers.

Some of the trucks could carry one type of thing only. Others were "general purpose" or utility trucks that could carry almost anything at all. Some were coming from the other side of town; others had come all the way across the country. Some were as big as a house; others were not much bigger than a car.

All trucks have an engine and a place for the driver.

Most trucks also have a space for carrying loads. Trucks that carry large, heavy loads have big, powerful engines. Those that carry lighter items have smaller engines. Most large trucks have diesel engines that run on diesel fuel. Others run on gasoline.

Not every kind of truck is shown in this book, but we have tried to give you an idea of how many different kinds there are. We have also tried to show something special about how they work and what makes each one right for its job. It might be fun when you are riding in a car or standing on a street corner to see if you can spot any trucks that we have not shown. See if you can figure out what makes them special, too.

Potato Truck

This truck has just brought a load of potatoes from a farm to a warehouse. At the warehouse they will be packed in crates, put on a larger truck, and sent to a factory that makes potato chips.

The potatoes would be damaged if they were just dumped out, so a truck designed for unloading potatoes is used. The body of the truck is wide at the top and narrow at the bottom — like a funnel.

At the back of the truck is a trapdoor that the driver opens when it is time to unload the potatoes. A small motor turns a metal conveyor belt that gently tumbles them out of the truck and into a storage bin.

Beverage Truck

Almost every town has dozens of stores and restaurants where beer and soft drinks are sold. The trucks that deliver these drinks have to make many stops.

To make the driver's job easier, this beverage truck has five large compartments on each side. Each compartment has a separate door that slides up so the driver can get to the cases of soda needed at each stop.

Underneath the truck are two more compartments that hold only a few cases of soda. Another compartment behind the rear wheel holds a hand truck. The driver uses the hand truck to carry the heavy cases into the stores.

Tractor-Trailer

The most common kind of truck for long-distance hauling is the tractor-trailer. The tractor is the front part. That includes the driver's compartment, or "cab," and the engine. The engine, like the engines of most big trucks, is usually a diesel.

There are many different kinds of trailers that the tractor pulls, from the familiar long box-shaped truck body to the tanker body, flatbed, or even car carrier. Some tractors pull two trailers; these are known as tandem rigs.

To connect the two parts of the truck, the driver backs the tractor up to the trailer until a ring-shaped collar known as the fifth wheel locks onto the underside of the trailer. The driver then connects the lines that allow him to control the brakes and running lights on the trailer.

Trailers without a set of front wheels are called semitrailers. When the trailer is not connected to the tractor, its front end rests on heavy metal legs called landing gear. Once the trailer is hitched to the tractor, the landing gear is raised by means of a crank.

Flatbed Truck

Flatbed trucks are usually of the tractor-trailer variety. They can carry giant spools of wire, stacks of concrete blocks, or even rocket engines.

Large, heavy, or bulky items would be hard to load or unload from a truck with sides and a top. Instead, the load is lifted onto the truck by crane and fastened with heavy clamps, bolts, or cables. Since only the driver's cab has a roof, a big plastic or canvas sheet called a tarpaulin may be used to keep the load dry.

Moving Van

The moving van is designed to carry a wide variety of household items — everything from cartons of books to grand pianos. Padded mats on the inside of the van protect the furniture.

The van has to be packed very carefully to keep furniture from shifting around while the truck is moving. Straps attached to the walls are sometimes used to keep things in place.

Over long distances a very large van may move several families' belongings at one time. A smaller van, like this one, is used to move individual families over shorter distances.

Heavy-Equipment Carrier

Heavy-equipment carriers are usually tractor-trailer rigs. They are used to carry bulldozers, steam shovels, or other large, heavy machines. Although a bulldozer can move on its own, it cannot go very fast (only about ten miles per hour). Also, it is so heavy that its metal treads would make dents in the road. This bulldozer has just been brought to a place where someone is building a new home.

After parking the heavy-equipment carrier, the driver gets out and folds down the ramps at the back of the truck. The bulldozer operator, who arrived in his own car, climbs into the bulldozer and carefully backs it down the ramps and off the truck. The truck driver folds up the ramps and drives away, leaving the bulldozer and the operator to do their work. When the work is done, the truck driver will come back and take the bulldozer away.

Delivery Van

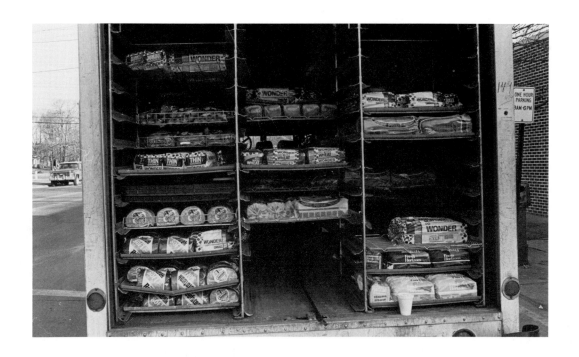

Delivery vans of many sizes and shapes are used to carry a wide variety of lightweight items — newspapers, dairy products, even the U.S. mail. This truck is bringing bakery products to supermarkets.

Goods are arranged on racks before the driver leaves on his route. That way the driver does not have to search for the correct items each time. When he arrives at one of his stops, he can get to the goods he needs from inside the front of the truck or he can go around to the back and open up a big sliding door. In either case, he loads the items onto a hand truck that he then wheels into the store. One person, the driver, can do everything.

Dump Truck

Dump trucks carry sand, gravel, rocks, soil, coal — anything that can be "dumped" without being damaged. This truck is carrying a load of sand.

The tailgate at the back of the truck is closed. When the driver is ready to unload, he pulls a lever that unlocks the tailgate. Another lever inside the cab starts up a pump that forces oil into two hollow cylinders called hydraulic pistons. The pressure of the oil forces the pistons to extend, the way a telescope opens up. The pistons force the body of the truck to tip over.

When the truck body tips, the weight of the sand forces the unlocked tailgate to open and the sand spills out.

Glass Truck

Large panes of glass that are used in picture windows and storefronts are very fragile and must be handled carefully. Special glass trucks are used to move them.

The sheets of glass rest on narrow ledges that run along the outside of the truck. The glass also leans against the slanted sides of the frame of the truck. Rubber-edged bumpers, which can be tightened and loosened, hold the glass in place.

Ice-Cream Truck

Ice cream melts if it gets warm, so ice-cream trucks are always refrigerated. The refrigerator unit is at the bottom of the truck body, just behind the front wheel.

Ice-cream trucks make many stops along the delivery route. Like beverage trucks they have several compartments, each with a separate door. The driver can open one door at a time. This way the ice cream is sure to stay cold.

Cement Truck

Cement is a powder made of ground-up lime, clay, and sand. Mixed with water and allowed to dry, it becomes as hard as a rock and can be used to hold bricks and other kinds of building materials together. Concrete is made of cement, sand, gravel, and water. Dams, highways, bridges, tunnels, basements of houses, and even skyscrapers are often built of concrete.

Cement trucks are sometimes called "transit mixers." The barrel-shaped part of the truck slowly revolves and mixes the cement or concrete while the truck is in transit. "In transit" means on the way.

In the photograph on the left, a truck is backed up under a loading platform where as much as ten cubic yards of cement, sand, gravel, and water are being loaded through a funnel. When the truck arrives at its destination, the material is all mixed and ready to pour. Metal sections are fitted together to form a channel, or sluice, and the mixture slides down the sluice to the exact spot where it is needed.

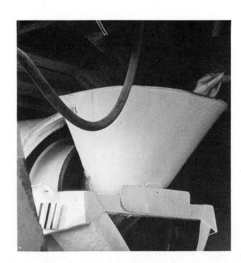

Tow Truck

Tow trucks are sometimes called wreckers because they are used to move cars and trucks that have been wrecked or damaged. This one is going to tow away a small van that has been in an accident.

First the driver backs the tow truck up close to the van. Then he takes two chains that are attached to the back of the truck and fastens them underneath the van. These chains are also attached to both sides of the tow bar. The tow bar is the flat piece that presses against the bumper of the van. It is connected to the back of the tow truck by a heavy metal pipe.

The photograph on the right shows a strong wire cable that runs over the boom and hooks to the tow bar. The engine of the truck powers a machine called a winch that reels the cable up, just as a fishing reel pulls in a line. The cable raises the tow bar, and the front wheels of the van are lifted off the ground. The van is ready to be towed away.

Garbage Truck

This truck is used to carry garbage and other kinds of waste material. The garbage is dumped into the large opening, or hopper, at the rear of the truck. Inside the hopper is a large blade attached to two hydraulic pistons. The blade crushes the garbage and forces it toward the front of the truck, making room for more.

Some garbage trucks are equipped to collect trash from large metal containers. The driver backs up to a container and attaches a strong hook to it. Using a power winch, the driver then tips the container over so the garbage spills into the truck. The container is then lowered to the ground and left behind to be filled up again.

Pickup Truck

In some rural areas of the United States more people own pickup trucks than passenger cars. The driver's compartment of a pickup truck is a lot like the inside of a passenger car, but there is no back seat.

Unlike many other trucks, pickups run on gasoline more often than diesel fuel. The back of the truck has an open area that can be used to carry small loads — lawn mowers, farm equipment, top soil, or brush cuttings. Most pickups have a tailgate that can be lowered to make loading and unloading easier.

Car Carrier

Car carriers deliver new cars to dealers who may be hundreds of miles from the automobile factories or from the ports where foreign cars arrive by boat. Stacking the cars on movable steel racks makes it possible to fit up to ten compact cars, eight full-size cars, or five vans onto a single carrier. The cars are chained or clamped down so they cannot roll around or fall off.

Off-loading the cars is as tricky as loading them. After reaching the destination, the driver removes a set of sturdy steel ramps from the side of the carrier and positions them at the rear. Hydraulic pistons raise or lower the racks with the cars on them until they are perfectly lined up with the ramps. The driver then unfastens the cars and carefully drives them off.

Since the carrier may be stopping at more than one dealer, the cars are loaded in reverse of the order in which they will be taken off.

Petroleum Tanker

Tanker trucks are used to carry many different petroleum products. The one on the opposite page picks up gasoline that arrives by barge and delivers it to local gas stations. The tank of the truck is divided on the inside into separate compartments. It can carry three different grades of gasoline — regular, premium, and unleaded — a total of 8,000 gallons. The gas from each compartment is pumped into a separate tank buried beneath the station.

The tanker above is bringing home-heating oil to the storage tanks behind the truck. Special valves underneath the tank of the truck allow the driver to pump different grades of heating oil into separate storage tanks.

Smaller tankers are used to draw the oil from the storage tanks and deliver it to individual homes. The driver unreels a hose from a compartment near the rear of the truck and inserts it into the opening of the home-storage tank. A meter on the pump in the truck keeps track of how much oil is delivered and how much remains in the truck.

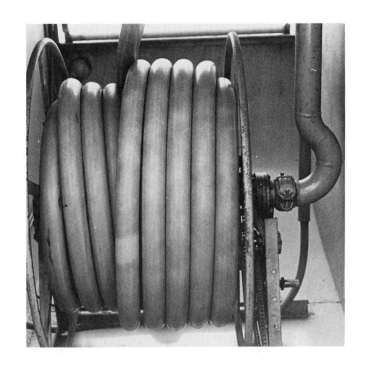

Fire Truck

There are many kinds of fire trucks, and each is used for a different purpose. Fire departments use ladder trucks, pumpers, personnel carriers, trucks that just carry water, and many combinations of these. The photographs show a general-purpose vehicle called an "attack" truck. It can carry 600 gallons of water to a fire and up to nineteen fire fighters. When hooked up to other water supplies, it can pump 1,250 gallons of water per minute through its eight hose connections. Fire axes, hand-held fire extinguishers, first-aid kits, and ladders hang on the side of the truck.

Individual hoses are controlled from a panel located behind the driver's cab. The levers and switches determine how much water comes out of each hose. The compartment on the right side of the truck holds a generator that can run electric lights or any other electrical equipment needed at the scene of a fire.

At the back of the truck one hundred yards of canvas fire hose is neatly folded and ready for use. Three people can ride to a fire standing on the rear platform.

Elevator-Platform Truck

This is a common type of truck used to deliver items like furniture or appliances.

The driver and his helper place a desk and filing cabinets on a platform at the rear of the truck. The driver then pushes a lever and a hydraulic piston gently lowers the platform to the ground. The furni-ture can then be rolled away on hand trucks.

When delivery is completed, the driver and his helper close the heavy metal door. With the help of the hydraulic piston they fold the platform underneath the back of the truck. They are ready to make another delivery.

About the Author

Ken Robbins is a former book editor who has been fascinated with trucks ever since he was a small boy. He spent several months traveling throughout New York State and New Jersey observing trucks in operation and taking the photographs for this book. Now a free-lance photographer, Ken Robbins lives in East Hampton, New York, with his wife.